Introduction

Rhyming strong
Instead
Watch the stars pass

Moon over Athens
Lights my way along the path
Follow old footsteps

LOVE

All is sex
Sell it
Television

In love with another
I am a bug on the move
"Forgive me, my love..."

Bring it home
Sing me
True and honest

LOVE

Pall of depression
A warm blanket of lost hope
See it and you'll weep

Armchair leg
High heels
Pussy pillow

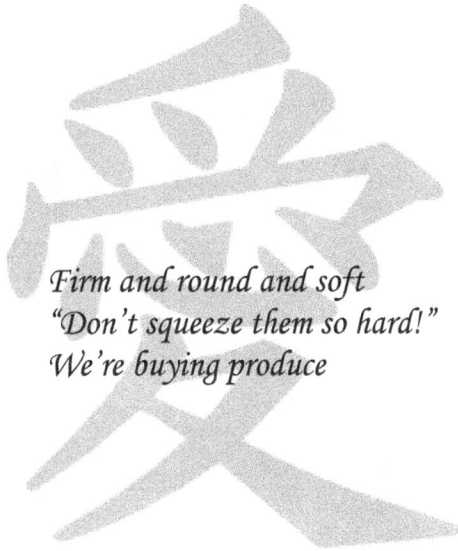

Firm and round and soft
"Don't squeeze them so hard!"
We're buying produce

LOVE

Poor Yorick
The sap
Just an old skull

Deep space psychosis
Darkness belies the expanse
Breathe deep the starlight

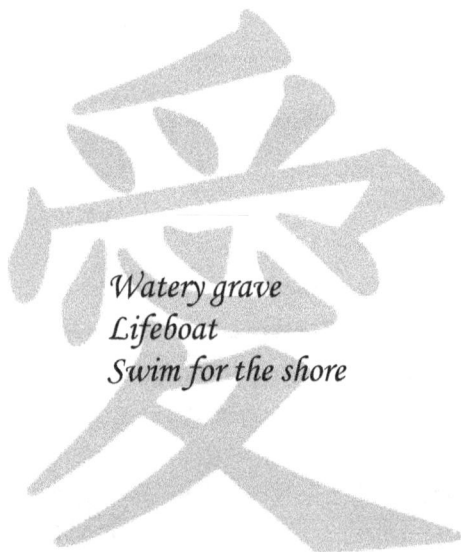

Watery grave
Lifeboat
Swim for the shore

LOVE

She nibbles my ear
I gently push her mouth off
"Give me back my corn!"

Yell my name
Echo
Answers itself

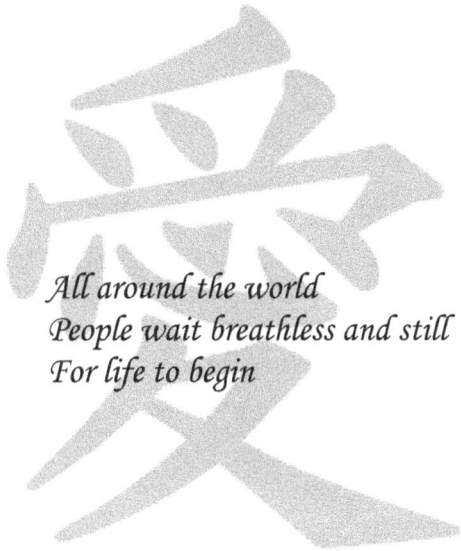

All around the world
People wait breathless and still
For life to begin

Bowling ball
Pins are
Nailed to the lane

Seeing all eating
Give a purpose to living
This is what life means

<u>*3-2-4 Beats*</u>

Heated breeze
Cross legs
Wishing for more

LOVE

Stop the pound
Cry stop!
Wipe the tears dry

Cartoon fun
Sleep now
No night needed

Pungent rug
Broken
Vacuum sits still

LOVE

Depressing
Assess
I pass the test

Words of hope
Today
Lost encounter

Cat is gone
Miss her
Back someday soon

LOVE

Not bereft
Loving
You and I see

Sitting spread
Ready
Soft, strong, heated

Lying flat
Tension
Waiting sweaty

LOVE

So, too, you
Little
Breaking my fast

Talons coy
Drop it
Yesterday gone

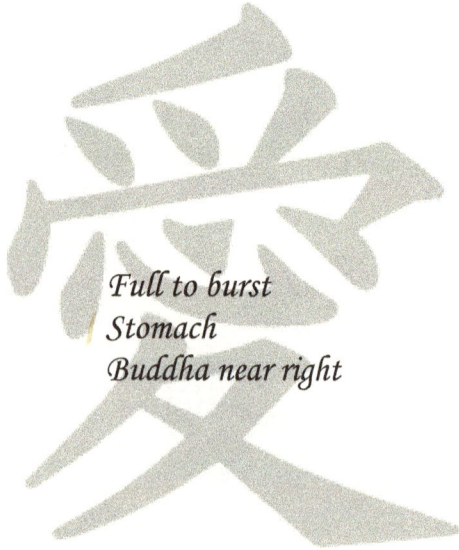

愛

Full to burst
Stomach
Buddha near right

LOVE

Funny man
Watch it!
Marbles punch line

Children sing
They should
We are old now

Serves you right
Assume
My love is gone

LOVE

Tag a beat
Unknown
Call me writer

Meat/ cheese bliss
Not food
Climb that sky wall

Nature song
Always
Sing forever

LOVE

Wisdom lost?
Never
Born with it, world

Cool, still, calm
Nature
Serene Action

Forever
Staying
Gone in no time

LOVE

Aggressive
Wanting
Burst reaction

Sighing loud
Coasting
Life diary

Sing for me
Useless
Your angry soul

LOVE

Days gone by
So long
Here now, present tense

Quid pro quo
Desire
Yours "No; mine "No"

I cause heat
Without
Even trying

LOVE

Mother's age
My response
Is best said old

Ancient dance
Always
Falls short of wish

Freakish claws
Growling
Words of real hope

LOVE

True courage
Catching
In spite of fear

The best day
Arms crossed
Love progressing

Stuck in bubble
Popping
Superheroes

LOVE

Innocent
Sweet face
Nothing really

Brainy girl
Cheering
Sporting event

Metaphor
No rhymes
Don't understand

LOVE

Pliant walls
Our mind
Only stops us

Perfect perk
Nipples
Bruised sideboob

Gold necklace
Stockings
Corset unbuttoned

LOVE

Afterwards
Calm smile
Resting sated

Summer heat
Homeless
Layered clothing

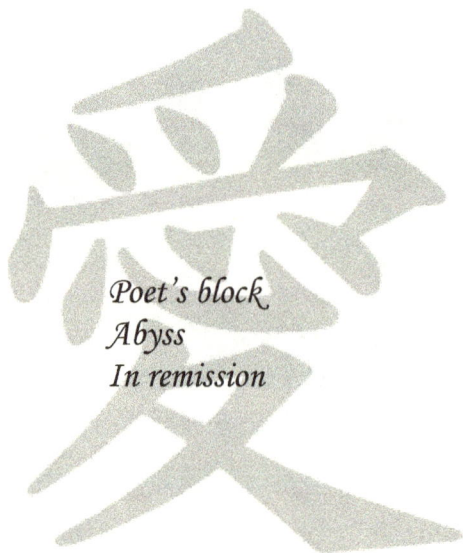

Poet's block
Abyss
In remission

LOVE

Sally forth
Persist
Nothing ending

Cute couple
Baby
Constant argue

T.v. face
Smiling
Living the dream?

LOVE

Testify
Soulful
Cream of mushroom

Ages past
'member
Joust to the death

Stern Equus
Bucking
Falling from on high

LOVE

Spears pointing
Dungeon
Such bad music

Mutton meal
Sheepish
Face turning red

Despairing
Captured
Parents are too

LOVE

Harmony
Boy band
No bass, their voice

Fantasy
Girl group
What is the point?

Braided wig
Thirty
Don't need disguise

LOVE

Serious
Facebook
Wants to have fun

Leads the pack
First wife
One of many

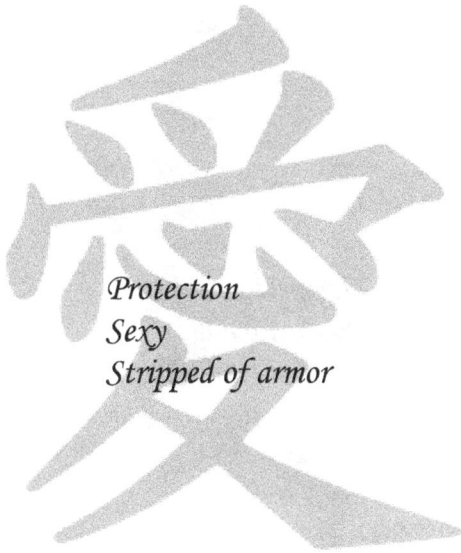

愛

Protection
Sexy
Stripped of armor

LOVE

Cross the lake
She's wet
What does it mean?

Butterfly
Don't move
Sits on blade edge

Tempered steel
Etched blade
Golden cord hilt

LOVE

Scales and fangs
Breathes fire
Basho's dragon

Bad-ass girls
Fighters
Leather jackets

Runway strut
Spiked heels
Sword on her belt

愛

LOVE

Swaying curves
Slight bounce
Curly brown hair

Sight to see
Don't blink
So many skirts

Lotion spread
Tan legs
Don't want to leave

LOVE

Legs are spread
Tan arms
I want to stay

Serious
Why not?
That's what life is

Call me sly
Cunning
Pick my nose clean

LOVE

Calling all cars!
Makes sense
If cars are phones

Bratwurst dog
Baseball
Brown mustard cat

Mirrored shades
Her eyes
I see myself

LOVE

I like food
So strange
Food likes me too

Do they hurt?
Tattoos
Now, don't you cry

Senseless
Just watch
Silly stupid

LOVE

Snap my food
Send it
Looks delicious

Bottom lip
Stretch it
Over your head

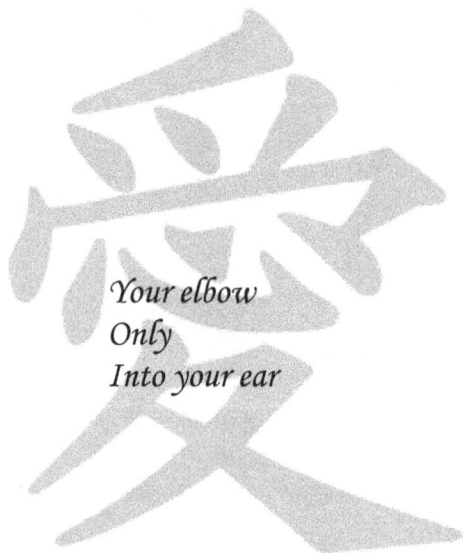

Your elbow
Only
Into your ear

LOVE

Calm the storm
Beach front
Twenty-foot waves

Strips and cheese
Before
Grilled hamburger

Triangle
Squared line
Circle no end

LOVE

Prancing pants
See her
Mine start dancing

First chances
Starring
Insecurities

Pluck them slow
Heartstrings
Inspiration

LOVE

Words of love
My soul
Penned in lyrics

Uplifting
Soul songs
Feed my soul fire

Sing my heart
Tuneful
Bass and treble

LOVE

A good beat
Feel it
My heart's concert

Celebrate
Dancing
To my heart-drums

Can it work?
Will it?
Lyrical path

LOVE

July heat
Matches
Songs of my heart

Sitting here
Writing
Red bump flea bites

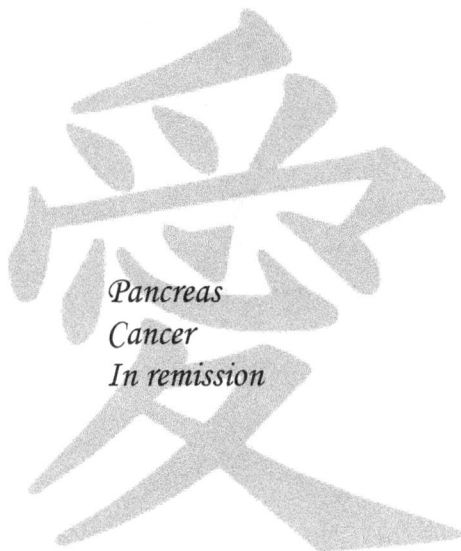

Pancreas
Cancer
In remission

LOVE

Battle scars
Torn up
Cancer weapons

Eating now
Wasn't
For a long time

愛

Sell me stuff
Movie
Silent preview

LOVE

It's all good
Music
New and old beats

Frontline look
Firestorm
World in terror

Pigs can't fly
Guess what?
Now they can talk

LOVE

Blue pink red
Out there
Bring it back home

Numbered balls
Alone
Single bingo

Pyramids
Old, dry
Strong history

LOVE

Rich in wealth
Go back
Ancient lessons

Ancient ways
Plural
Gods of nature

From the start
Way back
People don't change

LOVE

Standing firm
Nerve meat
Tickle me right

Awesome flat
Perfect
So into me

Atmosphere
Simple
Dusk like dark dawn

愛

LOVE

Small portions
Bursting
Lots of money

I don't dine
Portions
I eat instead

愛

Variety
Enjoy
Counter flavors

LOVE

Opposites
Gourmet
Salty sweet fat

Recognize
Flavors
Synchronize tastes

Seasoned meat
Spicy
Tears to my eyes

LOVE

Escargot
What? Huh?
Are you kidding?

Fast food fiend
Common
One of the crowd

愛

Oh, I say!
Darling
Salad fork, left

LOVE

All the rage
Trending
For five minutes

What the hell?!
Grilling
Antelope balls

Sour cream
Chocolate
Sinfully good

LOVE

Spoken loud
Her point
She thinks I'm deaf

More money
Love it
Exciting fun

Strong as hell
Didn't know
I could endure

LOVE

Life past it
Open
Much better now

Translucent
Pallid
Reduced hemo

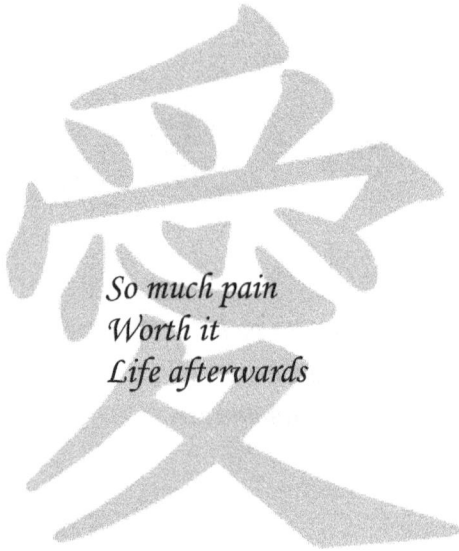

So much pain
Worth it
Life afterwards

LOVE

Food perfect
After
I.v. tube meals

Following
Cancer
Surgery dazed

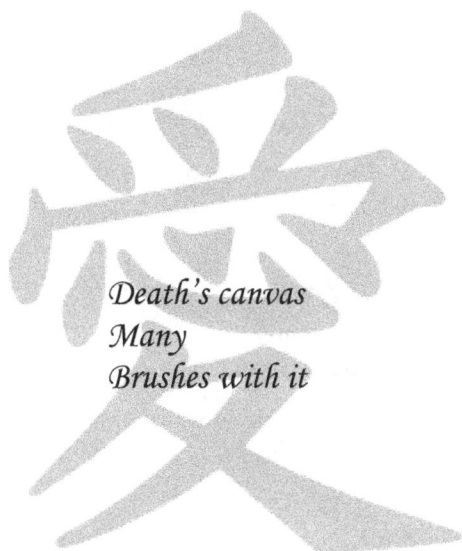

Death's canvas
Many
Brushes with it

LOVE

Pancreas
Cancer
Ridiculous

Remission
Beat it
My doctor knights

Very weak
No more
Severe blood loss

LOVE

Years of pain
Gone by
Carcinoma

Life on hold
Rotting
Healed by doctors

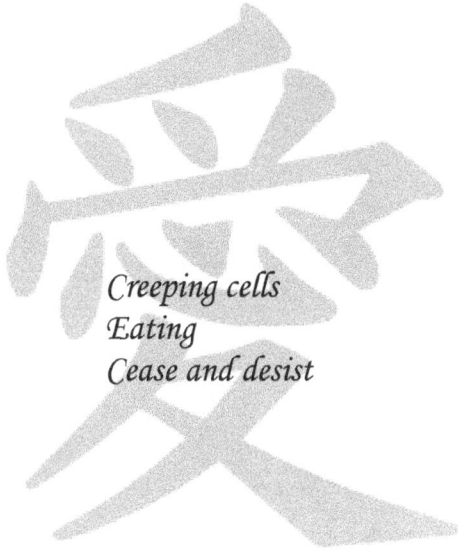

Creeping cells
Eating
Cease and desist

LOVE

So much time
So few
Hands for it all

愛

Intermission

LOVE

5-7-5 Beats

Vedic sages sing
Bodhidharma knew full well
Beatific smile

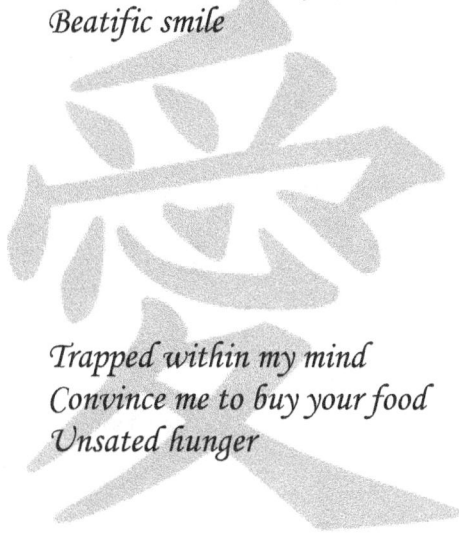

Trapped within my mind
Convince me to buy your food
Unsated hunger

LOVE

In love with another
I am a bug on the move
"Forgive me, my love..."

Torn and soiled hat
A gift from a love of mine
Stolen from a corpse

A cat on the prowl
Caterwauling on a fence
Fur and claws videoed

LOVE

Wrestling with fate
Put the blame where blame is due
Pollen on the wind

Await guillotine
My crime is one of good deeds
the sun burns my neck

Well-worn writing desk
Graffiti with a pen knife
Termites eat their fill

LOVE

Face against a rock
Clouds of epidermal spring
The rock wears my smile

Running up some steps
Time is not against me now
Summer steals my sweat

Wearing a jester's hat
Halloween clothes everywhere
All the year round

LOVE

Time to sell my soul
Yet another bad offer
July heat calms me

Sorry for the mess
Play your song for my parents
Your music sings spring

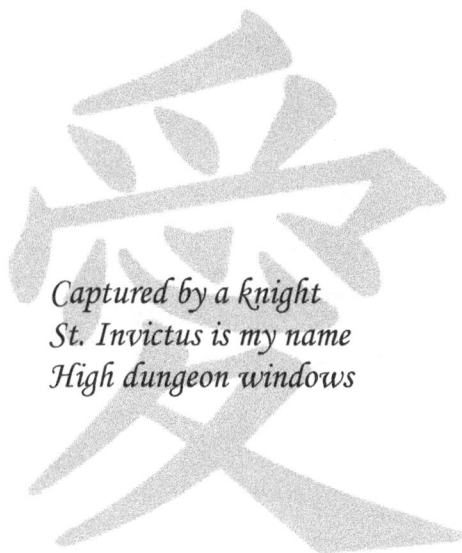

Captured by a knight
St. Invictus is my name
High dungeon windows

LOVE

Gold butterfly dust
Silver firefly aether
Jade hummingbird wings

See me seeing you
A flash of jet-black cotton
I'm red with summer

Call me heart bereft
Desire your skin's surf and turf
Warmth for my winter

LOVE

Why no children yet?
I am a big kid myself
Think too much just me

Why the long face, horse?
Are you tired of the saddle?
Your bridle too tight?

愛

Fourth of July passed
Grills are cold and parties done
Independence gone

LOVE

Don't understand it
What is this show selling me?
Strange television

July heat is intense
In the battle for comfort
July is winning

愛

Summer remembered
Now I have electric breeze
Past summers killed me

LOVE

Faces I don't know
What are they discussing now?
Life in all its ways

I only wonder
Are these words a new career?
Or just a hobby?

Sitting by myself
Me, myself and I
Just my life called hope

LOVE

Sex, love, what's the diff?
It is easy to explain
Your care and concern

Pet gone forever
Another loving creature
Only a cat, right?

High up in a tree
Granddad throws down old pears
Storm waves crash

LOVE

My lonely old pants
Pursue a different crevice
Stupid old trousers

Shrew bitch gold-digger
Why do I put up with it?
You in lingerie

Yellow-golden sand
Covers my feet every step
In an hour glass

LOVE

Lonely droning bee
Wears a dress of white lily
Lining the asphalt

See me home safe, girl
I'll show you my gratitude, girl
You left too soon, girl

Always on top
Sweating under the covers
Bunk beds are fun

LOVE

Muscles singing loud
A cry of "My god! Don't stop!"
Much needed rub-down

Breathing in her air
Our bodies smelling so strong
Car fan is broken

She grabs it, sighing
I feel the pain in my hips
"Give me back my wallet"

LOVE

Stretched out, full to burst
Holding liquid I shoot in
A water balloon

Late night gaming gain
Green and greedy game gain get
Pc gaining game

Mirrored shades hide soul
Wide flow shoulders tapered waist
Bottom steel panties

LOVE

Kick ass in high heels
Not a hair out of place, girl
Grab my sword for me

Simple times, my mind
Not for me, those complex thoughts
Thinking wears me out

Kick that leg higher
Show everything you've got
All that you can do

LOVE

Must tweet everything
My life is fascinating
Not boring at all

July heat continues
Feeling drained of energy
Fleas are peppy, though

Gothic lipstick spikes
Talons made of estrogen
Curvy, creepy sex

LOVE

Must be personal
Yet apply to everyone
It's confusing, right?

Pop goes the easel
Sing a song of time spent
Bling abounds with posing

Silly stupid fun
The lead doesn't always win
Fairness in action

LOVE

Boarding the Metro
Rumbling above the train tracks
Forgot my ticket

Always on the lookout
Finding my muse everywhere
A patchwork of song

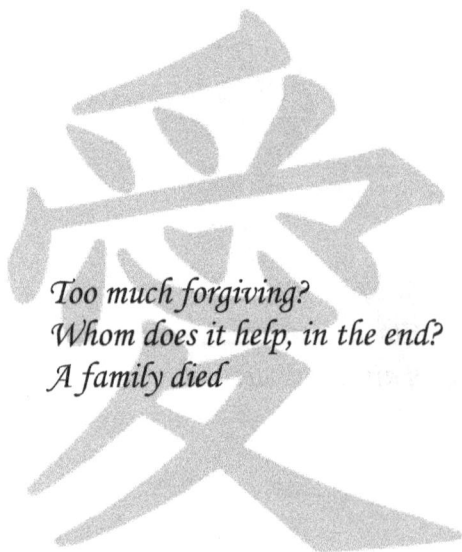

愛

Too much forgiving?
Whom does it help, in the end?
A family died

LOVE

What the hell is it?
A living, breathing fog bank
The thud of its pulse

You drink with wet lips
My rod is at an angle
As we try to fish

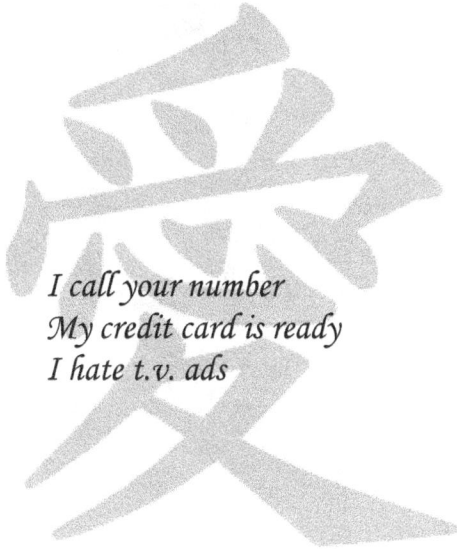

I call your number
My credit card is ready
I hate t.v. ads

LOVE

Two pussies at home
They're tough and fun and are mine
Fur is everywhere

Nature's vast array
Paint the canvas of my soul
An apt simile

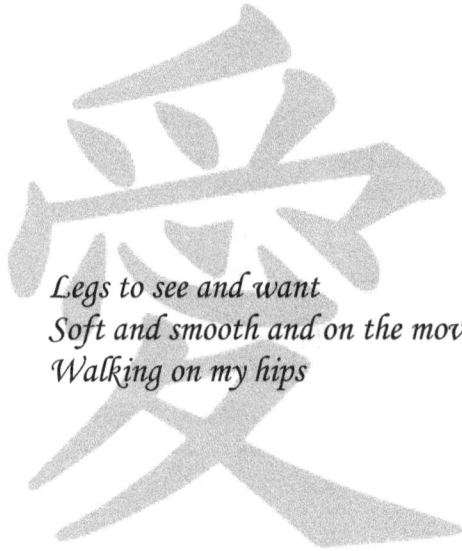

Legs to see and want
Soft and smooth and on the move
Walking on my hips

LOVE

Breasts to make me drool
Moist and sweet and delicious
Fire roasted chicken

Curly tangled bush
A sweetly scented flower
Thorns prick my fingers

Your scent draws me near
A musk of thick and sweet air
Perfume counter girl

LOVE

A tale of my city
So much movement near my home
Makes the world go round

So, I'm not a prude
I likes me the girls
More about my life

Spanish dancing girl
You flamenco through my mind
And leave me sated

LOVE

Girl with a Mohawk
Beautiful, tough and naked
I dream I'm your choice

Heels and panties
Like a magnet for my cock
She wears nothing else

Always a lady
Coy and smiling at my heart
You see me melting

LOVE

"My god. What a dick!"
"Never seen such a pussy!"
We're having a fight

Bobbing up and down
She glistens with drops of sweat
She loves her push-ups

"Not so hard, baby!"
"Which head should I stroke first,
love?"
Playing the bongos

LOVE

Passing the hours
I love the computer screen
A park down the street

Big, wide world outside
Early years spent wandering
Now I love four walls

A day of laundry
Adding soap and softener
To me or my clothes?

LOVE

Love the overcast
Doesn't bring depression, no
Atmospheric air

Battled with cancer
My pancreas the enemy
Doctor knights triumphed

To battle stations
Incoming cancer bomb shells
I'm scarred from the fight

LOVE

Claws, fangs, drooling hate
Bloody ripped and torn bodies
Beast from outer space

School girl sleepover
Painted nails and winsome smiles
Plotting mankind's downfall

Calling me to them
Twenty is all the rage
Buffalo hot wings

LOVE

Round, sleek, crafted face
Hands moving smooth and precise
Brand new gold Swiss watch

Teaching kids lessons
Friendship, caring and humor
Some t.v. is great

Teach all tolerance
Show the next generation
Global unity

LOVE

Living my small life
Going about my day-to-day
Ignoring the clouds

I bought a new watch
I'm proud of the way it looks
Isn't that funny?

愛

Fear descends on all
Shadows over the city
Cries and dire echoes

LOVE

Some want to see ghosts
Fear is excitement with dread
Life in the darkness

Disembodied voice
Crying for help from beyond
Imagination

Watching for spirits
Seeing what we want to see
Excitement and fun

LOVE

Creepy foreboding
Walking slowly towards the sound
Wait and you will see

Calling to the dead
Sadness, loss and no return
We hope it's not us

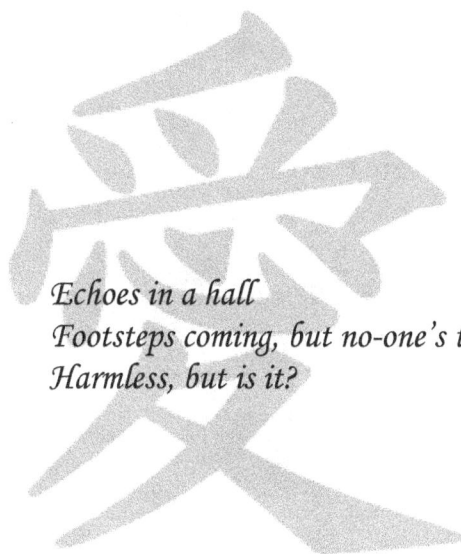

Echoes in a hall
Footsteps coming, but no-one's there
Harmless, but is it?

LOVE

Hyper-excitement
A voice on a recorder
Shocking, stunning fun

Don't you believe it
We hope to experience
Look to death when bored

Back into sunlight
Warm, gentle and full of hope
A cricket chirping

LOVE

Perfect for growing
A huge expanse of nature
Ripples on a lake

As big as outdoors
Free of claustrophobia
Makes us want to run

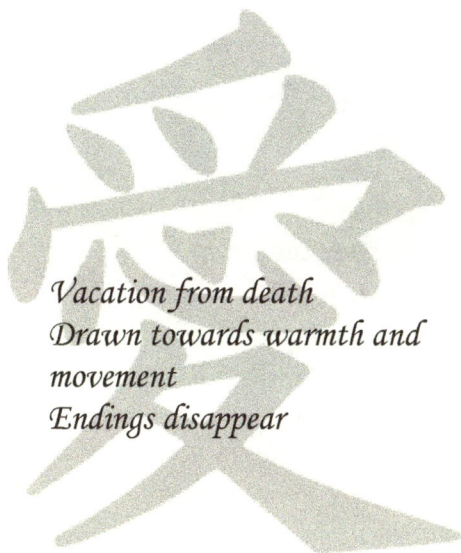

Vacation from death
Drawn towards warmth and
movement
Endings disappear

LOVE

Pain is distracting
It pulls our focus towards it
Life is diminished

Quality of life
Movement inside and out
Thinking and feeling

Answer the phone
See who's on the other end
Is it your purpose?

Pleated skirt bouncing
Flashes of colored cotton
Moth to a bon fire

Again about girls
My gaze is so drawn thither
Seeing orgasm

Sports fun eludes me
Not macho enough, I guess
My bookstore loves me

LOVE

Late dark-purple dusk
Shading closer to the night
Quiet window light

Stacks of green, coin piles
Easily gotten by some
Me, not so much

Turning a profit
Thick, fat stacks in my wallet
At least, that's the dream

LOVE

Making snow angels
Arms and legs sweeping an arc
Gold\green money snow

Photo of my food
Steak, eggs, tacos, pasta, cake
Written on paper

Mild summer this year
No desiccating heat yet
A nice break from sweat

愛
LOVE

Honeysuckle arch
Huntington Beach house back yard
Home where I grew up

www.ingramcontent.com/pod-product-compliance
Lightning Source LLC
Chambersburg PA
CBHW020514030426
42337CB00011B/381